The Adventures of Ace the Face

**SHERRY CULPEPPER
&
ACE THE FACE**

Copyright © 2019 Sherry Culpepper & Ace The Face
All rights reserved
First Edition

PAGE PUBLISHING, INC.
New York, NY

First originally published by Page Publishing, Inc. 2019

ISBN 978-1-64462-308-4 (Paperback)
ISBN 978-1-64462-309-1 (Digital)

Printed in the United States of America

Prelude

Hi, everyone! It's me, Ace. For those of you who don't know me yet, let me introduce myself. I am an American Pocket Bully. In other words, I'm a big brown dog. Lots of people call me Ace the Face because they say I make a lot of funny faces. I don't quite get that because it's the only face I have!

I'm lying in my big comfy bed, thinking back over the last year, and all of the crazy things that brought me here to my forever home. The craziest thing of all was a big, bad storm called Hurricane Irma. Let me tell you all about why it was the worst thing and the best thing that ever happened to me!

Puppy Days

I don't remember much about being a little puppy. But what I do remember is that I had people who loved me, and I loved them too. Some of them were tall, and a few were short people called kids, and the short ones were fun to play with! There was a lot of laughing and playing and rides in their truck. The people taught me never to go to the bathroom in my kennel and to never bite or hurt anybody. They always said I was a good boy, but just a little crazy. But they loved me anyway.

Then suddenly, everything changed. The changes started the first time I heard the words "Hurricane Irma," and it was really scary!

Hurricane Coming

When things started to change, I noticed that my people were acting different. They were worried instead of happy, and all they talked about was "the storm." Its name was Irma and it was headed right at the Florida Keys, and that's where we live! My tallest person told me that we all had to move to safe places where the wind and rain from Hurricane Irma couldn't hurt us. My safe place would be the electric company where he worked. (That's the place that keeps the lights on in the dark, and lots of other important stuff.) So, he packed up my kennel and away we went.

There were lots of people staying at the electric company during the storm, so they would be safe. There were tall people, short people, and even some other dogs, and one black-and-white cat. All the people visited me, so I liked it there. I didn't know that because of Irma, it would be my home for a long, long time.

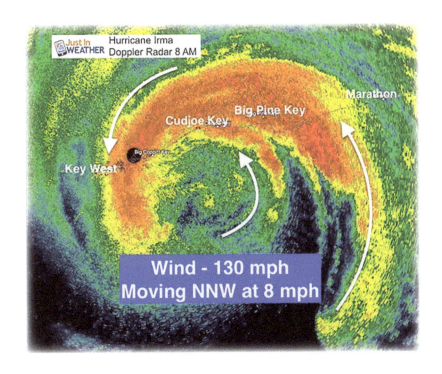

Scary Night

It was a very scary night when Hurricane Irma hit! There were lots of loud noises and I was afraid. But the people kept checking on me, and that helped a lot. I thought that night would never end! But it finally did, and we were all okay. I got to get out of my kennel and go outside to go to the bathroom. I couldn't stop running around! I was only a year old, and I had lots of energy! But way too soon, I had to go back in my kennel. Most of the people had to get to work because Key West and the Florida Keys got hit very hard by Hurricane Irma, and the electric was off everywhere, and they had to start fixing everything. Yep, Hurricane Irma changed a lot of people's lives, including mine. Many people lost their homes. I soon found out that things would never be the same again!

The Old Man

The days after the hurricane all went by in kind of a blur. The people that worked at the electric company are called linemen. Their job was to get the lights back on for everyone. My person was one of those guys. They worked constantly back then, even in the dark, every single day and night. Lots of the linemen people stayed there all the time because their houses were too messed up to live in. That's what happened to my person and me too. Then he started staying with friends with good houses, but I couldn't go with him. The weeks and months went by and I figured this place would be my home and the linemen staying there would be my family. But one by one they all left to go back to their homes. And soon, at night, I was alone there in my kennel.

Every morning, the whole crew would visit me before they left in their big trucks. But one old man was always there first to see me. He brought blankets and pillows (which I always ripped up) and treats and bones. He always talked to me when he took me for my walks. He told me that his dog had died that year and he missed him so much. He told me that being with me made him feel better. It was the beginning of a beautiful friendship.

Homeless

The old man never missed a day visiting me, even when he didn't have to work there that day. He showed up every morning to take me for a walk and spend time with me. On those days, he brought an old lady with him to visit me. She loved to hug me and she laughed all the time. She gave me the name Ace the Face.

Those were my favorite days.

Then my person told me that I couldn't stay at the electric company anymore because they have "rules". The storm was over and everybody had to go home. The trouble was, I didn't have a home to go to anymore! So he'd take me with him to stay at other people's homes for a while, but most people didn't have room for a big crazy brown dog! He was very sad because he had no place to keep me. That's the first time I heard the word "adopt".

He told me he found a good family to adopt me and that meant to keep me safe forever! I was scared and tired of moving around from place to place. But would my new family love me, and would I love them?

When the new people came through the door to come get me, my tail would not stop wagging! It was the old man and old lady! And I knew that when they adopted me, we would love each other forever! I knew they would always keep me safe

My Forever Home

And so, my new adventure began.

All of a sudden, I was living in a real house with my own family. I will admit that I had a little trouble adjusting in the beginning. There were a few "incidents" of peeing on the couch. I sure loved all these big white fluffy things called pillows. I ripped up dozens of them, and there was stuffing all over the house! I chewed up a few shoes and remote controls back then too. But I learned to be a good boy, because the old man and the old lady love me and always forgive me when I am bad. I am a so happy living in my forever home. I am a very lucky dog.

So always remember that even when you go through the worst of times like I did with that big hurricane, that sometimes the worst thing that ever happens to you, could end up being the best thing that ever happens to you.

Love,

Ace

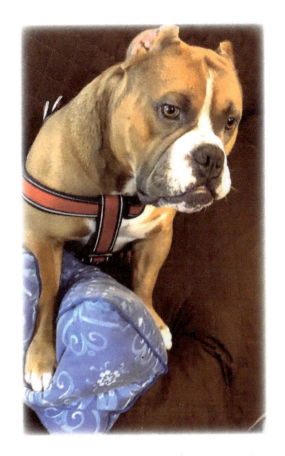

About the Author

Sherry Culpepper was born a coal miner's daughter and was raised in the hills of Western Pennsylvania. But she never felt at home in her own backyard. She always longed for warm weather and palm trees. When she first visited Key West, Florida, in the spring of 1970, she knew immediately that she had found her true home. And so, she made a life for herself on that little island. She especially loved the Atlantic Ocean, and her happiest days were spent in that crystal blue water. She met many wonderful, adventurous people in Key West, and was especially intrigued by the hunters of treasure! Many Spanish galleons sank off the Florida Keys in the 1600s and 1700s. Some of her closest friends found millions of dollars in coins and artifacts from those shipwrecks, and relied on Sherry to educate people about these treasures, and offer them for sale. It was an exciting career path, which she still enjoys to this day! But through all her life, Sherry has had a deep love for another kind of treasure, and that is her love of animals. She has had countless dogs and cats, and even rabbits throughout her life. Her latest "treasure" is a bulldog named Ace, adopted after Hurricane Irma in 2017. And he has quite a story to tell!

CPSIA information can be obtained
at www.ICGtesting.com
Printed in the USA
BVHW051111180319
542960BV00011B/1174/P